RHYTHM SECTION/CONDUCTOR

JAZZ IMPROVISATION SERIE

APPROACHING THE STANDARDS

by Dr. Willie L. Hill, Jr.

PREFACE

There are two groups of standards that help form the basic repertory used in jazz improvisation. The first group was created by jazz musicians directly from improvisation, experimentation and the analysis of musical forms, ideas and practices that were developed through study and the natural gifts of some of the greatest musicians of the twentieth century. This group codified jazz into chronological styles and provides concrete examples of its styles and concepts. The second group of standards is comprised of compositions written as popular songs during the first half of the twentieth century. Many of the composers of these songs were highly influenced by jazz composers and players. Jazz musicians also used compositions by composers who were not influenced by jazz because those compositions became excellent vehicles for jazz improvisation when the melodies were altered to fit jazz concepts.

In this series, Dr. Willie Hill has utilized compositions from both groups to give musicians a well-balanced selection of music to help the "fearful to the fearless" improve their jazz skills. He has provided a learning situation that is similar to a typical jazz gig setting and has included clearly written musical examples to demonstrate how an improvised solo might be constructed.

Every improviser is a composer who makes up melodies spontaneously. The model choruses give examples that can be studied, learned, broken into independent phrases and used to create other melodies that reflect more clearly what the improviser wants to say musically. Dr. Hill has given the player who uses this series an inside look at the jazz vocabulary, transcription opportunities, informative composer insights and a useful discography to help put the music into the context that is needed to improve his/her jazz skills. Whatever your instrument, you can have fun and learn a lot as you study the music, learn the melodies and play along with the excellent musicians on the enclosed CDs.

Dr. Billy Taylor

Editor: Pete BarenBregge
Production Coordinator: Edmond Randle
Technical Editor: Glyn Dryhurst
Finale Engraver: Mark Burgess
Art Design: Joe Klucar
Art Layout: María A. Chenique
Arranger: Ethan Neuburg

TABLE OF CONTENTS

INTRODUCTION

Approaching the Standards, Volumes 1, 2 and 3, are part of the Jazz Improvisation Series. From the jazz novice to budding professionals, this play-along series is designed to help individuals build a melodic, harmonic and rhythmic jazz vocabulary. Eight classic jazz standards are featured in each book and play-along CD for students to listen, analyze, transcribe and commit to memory. Each tune gives the player the opportunity to hear the jazz language performed by professional musicians as if they were performing at a real gig.

The Rhythm Section/Conductor book provides separate written parts for piano, bass and drums to accompany the C/B♭/E♭/Bass Clef books. *Multiple copies of this book are recommended for piano, bass and drums.* Similar to what is performed on the included CD, these written-out parts will allow *Approaching the Standards* to be performed with a live rhythm section. Although these written parts are intended to be used in a setting independent of the CD, the players are encouraged to listen to the CD for demonstration and reference to the jazz concept and interpretation. In addition to the piano, bass and drum parts, you will find great solo examples to listen to and imitate. Also included are composers' insights, transcription opportunities, a discography, a list of common jazz terms and lots of "licks and tricks" to assist you in the process of internalizing the jazz language. Have fun memorizing these classic jazz standards.

For the *piano player,* each of these jazz standards has a suggested piano part written for the head. For the solo sections, suggested chord voicings along with rhythms for comping are provided. Please bear in mind that these examples are only suggested voicings and rhythms and that there are unlimited variations. Basic chord progressions were used throughout these books to make it easier for the student to read. In many cases, chord extensions and alterations, particularly on the dominant chords, were written to capture the jazz flavor of each tune and to establish solid jazz voicings. Therefore, the written notes may extend beyond the notated chord progression. For the *bass player,* a suggested bass line for the head is written out and the chord changes are provided for the solo section. For the *drummer,* a suggested drum part for the head and one measure of a time pattern for the solo section are provided. For *guitar* players, chord frames are included in this book (and in the C book), and performance suggestions are included in the conductor's notes. For the *conductor,* specific tips, ideas and suggestions are provided with each jazz standard. To further your studies, Warner Bros. Publications offers many other fine jazz education books and materials pertaining to piano, bass, drums, guitar and jazz pedagogy.

CD icons are included to clarify the sequence of tracks in the book; observe the following:

A. First track for each tune
1. Head (demo)
2. Example improvisation (listen/analyze)
3. Improvised solo (listen/transcribe)
4. Head (demo)

B. Second track for each tune
1. Head (play along)
2. Solo choruses (create your own improvisation)
3. Head (play along)

I would like to acknowledge the support of the many individuals who have contributed time and creative energy to this series containing improvisation materials. Thanks to the efforts of Pete BarenBregge for his incredible guidance, insight and musicianship; to Bob Dingley for his inspiration, guidance and support; to Larry Clark for his vision during the early stages of development; to Bob Montgomery for his jazz arranging talent; to Shelly Berg, Ron Jolly and Javon Jackson for great written improvisations; to Paul Glessner for his research and advice; and special thanks to Willie Thomas for writing excellent improvisations and his role in helping conceive this project. To each of them I extend my sincere gratitude. Thanks to these fine musicians: Chris Vadala, Tim Leahey, Jamie Way, Ron Elliston, Dallas Smith, Paul Wingo and Clyde Conner.

NOTE: The collection of jazz riffs, rhythm patterns, harmonic concepts and much more were modeled after Willie Thomas' JAZZ ANYONE…? series (published by Warner Bros. Publications) in the preparation of materials presented in this book. Enjoy!

Dr. Willie L. Hill, Jr.

Dr. Willie L. Hill, Jr., is director of the Fine Arts Center at the University of Massachusetts-Amherst and a professor in music education. He received his B.S. degree from Grambling State University and earned M.M. and Ph.D. degrees from the University of Colorado-Boulder. He is currently president of the International Association of Jazz Educators (IAJE), president-elect of the Southwestern Division of the Music Educators National Conference (MENC), a member of the writing team for MENC's Vision 2020 and a member of the national board of directors for Young Audiences, Inc. Dr. Hill was a professor in music education and the assistant dean at the College of Music at the University of Colorado-Boulder for eleven years and director of education for the Thelonious Monk Institute. Prior to his tenure at the University of Colorado, Dr. Hill taught instrumental music and was music supervisor for 20 years in the Denver Public Schools. Professional performances in the Denver area include the Denver Broncos Jazz Ensemble, the Denver Auditorium Theater, Paramount Theater and as a freelance performer with Liza Minnelli, Lena Horne, Lou Rawls, Ben Vereen, Lola Falana, Johnny Mathis, Sammy Davis Jr., Dizzy Gillespie and many others. He is the founder and co-director of the Rich Matteson-Telluride Jazz Academy and former faculty member and woodwind specialist at the Clark Terry Great Plains Jazz Camp and the Mile High Jazz Camp in Boulder, Colorado. In 1998, he was inducted into the Colorado Music Educators Hall of Fame. He is co-author of *Learning to Sight-Read Jazz, Rock, Latin, and Classical Styles* (Ardsley House Publishers, Inc.) and the author of *The Instrumental History of Jazz* (N2K, Inc.). Hill is listed in the first edition of *Who's Who Among Black Americans* and *Who's Who Among International Musicians.*

NOW'S THE TIME

PIANO

LISTEN AND ANALYZE HEAD — Track 1 JAZZ DEMO

PLAY THE HEAD — Track 2 PLAY ALONG

BY CHARLIE PARKER

MEDIUM UP-TEMPO SWING

Suggested Rhythms For Comping

Pattern A.)   Pattern B.)   Pattern C.)

SOLO SECTION - 4 CHORUSES

SUGGESTED VOICINGS FOR COMPING

Track 2
PLAY ALONG

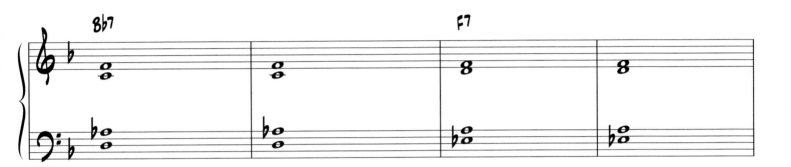

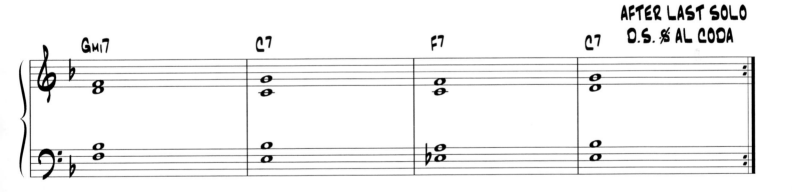

AFTER LAST SOLO
D.S. %. AL CODA

⊕ CODA

5

EXAMPLE IMPROVISATION
LISTEN AND ANALYZE
(JAZZ DEMO PLAYS 2 CHORUSES)

Track 1
JAZZ DEMO

BY WILLIE THOMAS

MEDIUM UP-TEMPO SWING

COMPOSER INSIGHT

NOW'S THE TIME

Charles Christopher Parker was born in Kansas City, Kansas, August 29, 1920, and died in New York City March 12, 1955. Nicknamed "Yardbird," shortened to "Bird," he is one of the most influential alto saxophonists to date. His stellar compositions include such jazz standards as "Now's the Time," "Scrapple From the Apple," "Ornithology," "Ko Ko," "Billie's Bounce," and a host of others. As one of the founding fathers and a master of bebop jazz, Bird performed in Kansas City in big bands, most notably the Jay McShann Orchestra and with various R&B and jazz groups. A traditional 12-bar blues, "Now's the Time" has a typical blues-style dominant 7th chord progression cycle. The dominant 7th chord is an action chord that sounds like it is always moving, never completely resolving. As with most blues tunes, you will need to focus on major, minor, and dominant scales/chords.

LICKS AND TRICKS

Lick #1 is a simple riff over the **I-IV-I** changes. Lick #2 is a blues riff with a syncopated rhythmical pattern. Lick #3 is a **I-VI-ii-V** two-bar turnaround that the player can superimpose over measures 11–12.

SCALES AND CHORDS

DISCOGRAPHY

NOW'S THE TIME
Charlie Parker - *Now's The Time* - Verve 825671
Charlie Parker - *Charlie Parker* - Verve 539757
Art Blakey - *A Night At Birdland Vol. 2* - Blue Note 46520
Sonny Rollins - *Greatest Hits* - RCA Victor 52062
Charlie Parker - *The Complete Charlie Parker On Verve* - Verve 837 141-2

NOW'S THE TIME

The tempo is 140 mm. This is a typical 12-bar blues chord progression, one of the most basic forms in western music. All (jazz) musicians should become familiar with the standard I-IV-V blues chord progression or, as it applies to this key, the F7-B♭7-C7 chord progression and the sequence of these chords. Listen carefully to the key or target measures 1–2, 4–5, 8–9 and 9–10 and examine the action of the dominant 7th chords. As the players begin to recognize this common progression, they will find themselves feeling comfortable improvising on the blues. Don't worry about keeping all eyes glued to the music for the blues chord progression. Instead, allow your students to use their ears and begin to learn to play the blues progression without music. The next step is to have the students learn to play the blues (without music) in all 12 keys! Try having the rhythm section set the groove or stretch out on this blues before the other wind instruments enter with the melody.

Piano:

- Piano and guitar should offer a simple and uncluttered comping style. With a rhythmical melody like this one, the rhythm section should offer a contrast to the melodic content.
- The three suggested rhythms for comping example patterns shown above the solo section are derived from rhythms played in the head. Use these patterns or devise similar patterns of your own.
- Piano and guitar need to be sensitive to each other with regard to conflicts of chord voicings and rhythm.
- Check out the suggested voicings and notice that the harmonic sound or quality is determined by the 3rd and 7th, **not** the root and 5th.
- Keep the voicings fairly simple with about 4–6 notes, and stay in the texture of the tune.

Bass:

- This tempo is ideal for the bass player. Dig in and sustain the energy from beginning to end.
- Work closely with the drummer's ride cymbal to keep the groove comfortable for the ensemble.
- Simplicity is the key to making this bass line swing. Play the root of the chord on the downbeat.
- You can add more colorful notes and add rhythmical variations as you become more experienced, but start out simple with your time as the first priority.
- The bass player's job in this musical setting is primarily to accompany, but work to shape your bass lines and develop melodically.
- Try recording the ensemble and listen to see if the bass lines are smooth and demonstrate good voice leading.

Drums:

- In this style of jazz, the drummer should complement or enhance the music, not overpower or dominate.
- The drummer has a few kicks in the head of the tune; after that, it's smooth sailing with basic swing time or the break-out pattern. The break-out pattern is only a general guide to what the drummer should play.
- Listen carefully to the CD recording to get a sense of how the drummer interprets the basic swing patterns.
- Kicks and hits that are quarter note or shorter should be played by snare; longer kicks use bass drum and cymbal.
- Use various cymbals to vary and refresh the sound, perhaps changing cymbals for each new soloist.

Guitar:

- Keep a simple and clean background comping style.
- The guitar player can enhance the overall ensemble time with various rhythmical comping patterns.
- If the introduction is extended or opened up, here is a chance to solo in this traditional swing style.
- As solo opportunities arise, think simple and develop solos gradually. Pace yourself.

SUGAR

PIANO

LISTEN AND ANALYZE HEAD · Track 3 JAZZ DEMO

PLAY THE HEAD · Track 4 PLAY ALONG

BY STANLEY TURRENTINE

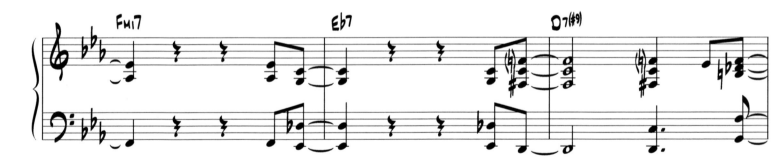

SUGGESTED RHYTHMS FOR COMPING

EXAMPLE IMPROVISATION
LISTEN AND ANALYZE
(JAZZ DEMO PLAYS 1 CHORUS)

C INSTRUMENTS

Track 3
JAZZ DEMO

BY JAVON JACKSON

COMPOSER INSIGHT

SUGAR

"Sugar" was written in an AB 16-bar song form by hard-bop tenor saxophonist, Stanley Turrentine, who was born in Pittsburgh, Pennsylvania, in 1934 and died in New York City, September 12, 2000. His style is rooted in blues, R&B, hard bop, and soul jazz. During the 1950s, he worked with the R&B band of Lowell Fulson, Earl Bostic, Max Roach, and others. Turrentine recorded as a leader during the '60s, '70s, and '80s with such musicians as Jimmy Smith, Shirley Scott, Tommy Flanagan, George Duvivier, George Benson, Gene Harris, and Grant Green. "Sugar," one of Turrentine's greatest hits, is a well-known groove tune with a melody line based on a minor pentatonic scale.

LICKS AND TRICKS

Lick #1 is a riff focused on the diminished chord, which adds color to the A section chord progression. Lick #2 is based on the blues scale and will work over the first eight bars of the tune. Lick #3 is an extended melodic and rhythmic pattern; use it over the second eight measures of the tune.

SCALES AND CHORDS

DISCOGRAPHY

SUGAR
Stanley Turrentine - *Best Of Mr. T* - Fantasy 7708

SUGAR

CONDUCTOR'S NOTES

The tempo is 106 mm. This is a clear example of what is known as a groove tempo. This fun tune has a great melody and a nice chord progression to improvise over. The first half is a minor progression with lots of ii-V chord progressions incorporating the half-diminished 7th chord; use the half-diminished scale. Using these minor chords allows some harmonic space to add color notes like the ninth as an example. The second half of the tune offers an opportunity to practice a sequence: a riff or motive transposed to fit different chords.

Piano:

- The half-diminished chord and the sharp ninth chord are critical to this chord progression; become familiar with their use and sound.
- At this moderate tempo, you can incorporate a few sustained chords.
- You can also freely add punctuated chords to add rhythmical energy and contrast.
- You can introduce and then resolve harmonic tension with the passing color tones, which will add forward motion.
- The three suggested rhythms for comping example patterns provided are derived from rhythms played in the head. Use these patterns or experiment on your own.
- The written tremolo effect is very effective, but use it sparingly.

Bass:

- A straight quarter-note walking line works best here.
- A rhythmical variation such as triplets or eighth-note groups can be used sparingly. Usually those effects are to add drive and energy to a swing feel.
- Observe the walking up or down to the next chord as it makes the bass line smooth and directs the band into the next chord. This is called voice leading.
- Remember to play the root of the chord change on the downbeat.
- Play straight ahead, and strive for tone.

Drums:

- Remember that the written drum part is only a break-out guide.
- A cross-stick on four will work nicely in this groove with some minimal fills at each turnaround.
- You will need to balance the energy flow in this tune; maintain the tempo yet stay relaxed.
- Listen carefully to the CD recording to get a sense of how the drummer interprets the basic swing patterns.
- Use various cymbals to contrast and refresh the sound, perhaps changing cymbals for each new soloist.
- Keeping the melody and chord progression in your mind is a rule everyone follows, but because this tune is only 16 bars, it's easy to get careless.

Guitar:

- "Sugar" requires a basic comping style of quarter notes in the mid-range.
- Try alternating choruses with the piano for contrast in color and style.
- Soloing on this tune will be fun. Keep a more traditional mellow jazz tone on your instrument.
- When called for, the jazz guitarist should strive to sound like an acoustic guitar.
- Always work *with* the piano player—not *against*. Stay in the mid-range of the instrument using primarily the top four strings.

HONEYSUCKLE ROSE

LISTEN AND ANALYZE HEAD — Track 5 JAZZ DEMO

PLAY THE HEAD — Track 6 PLAY ALONG

BY FATS WALLER

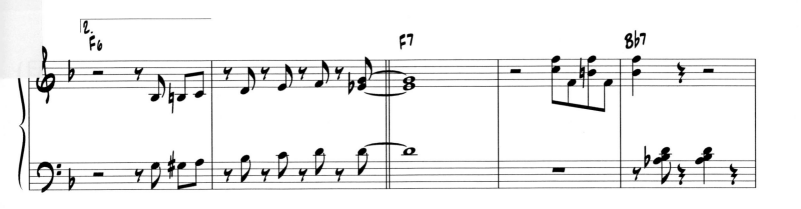

SUGGESTED RHYTHMS FOR COMPING

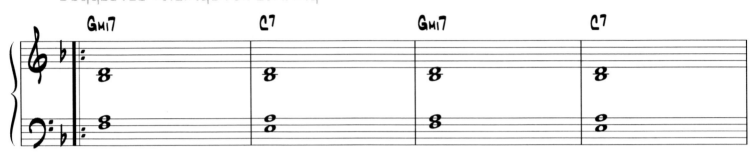

PATTERN A.)   PATTERN B.)   PATTERN C.)

SOLO SECTION - 2 CHORUSES
SUGGESTED VOICINGS FOR COMPING

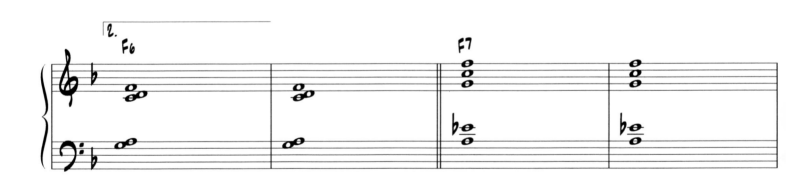

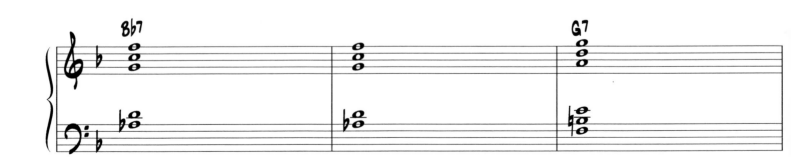

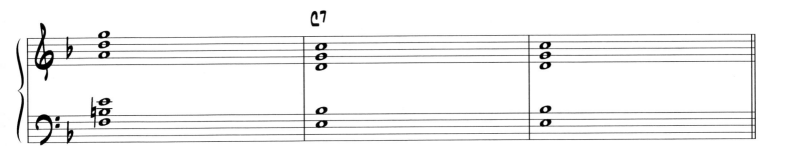

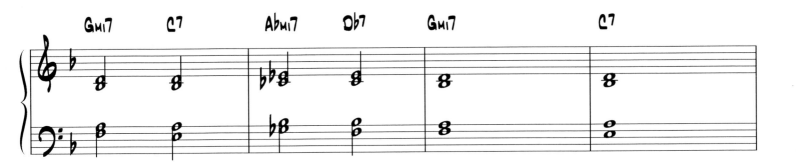

AFTER LAST SOLO
D.S. ⅀ AL CODA

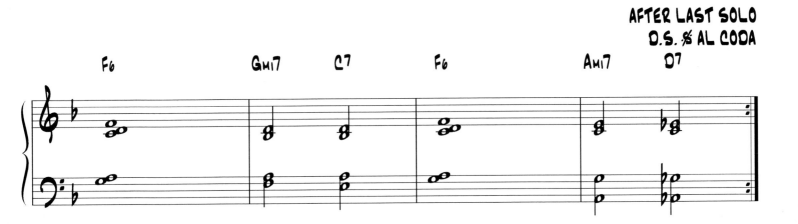

EXAMPLE IMPROVISATION
LISTEN AND ANALYZE

Track 5
JAZZ DEMO

(JAZZ DEMO PLAYS 1 CHORUS)

BY RON JOLLY

IMPROVISED SOLO
LISTEN, ANALYZE AND TRANSCRIBE 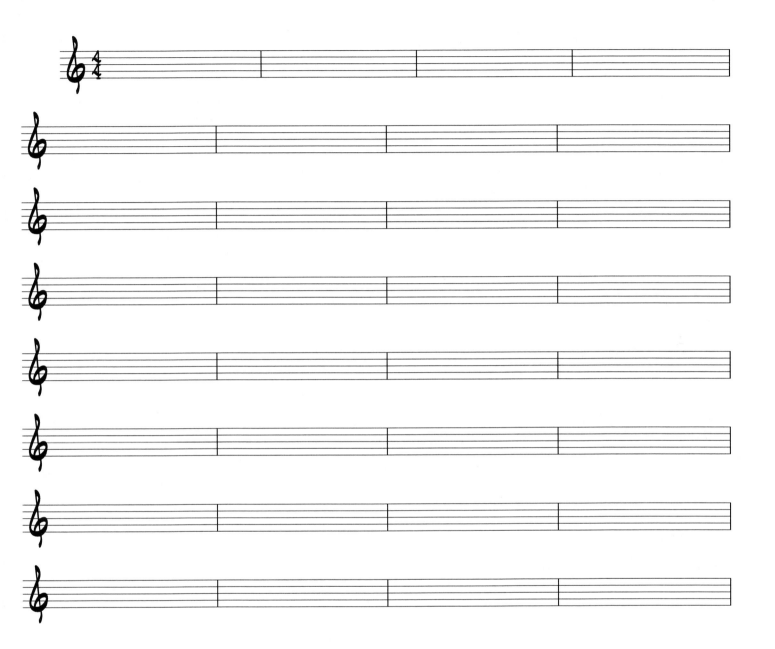 Track 5
JAZZ DEMO
(JAZZ DEMO PLAYS 1 CHORUS)

COMPOSER INSIGHT

HONEYSUCKLE ROSE

This AABA 32-bar song form was composed by Thomas Wright Waller, affectionately known as Fats. He was born in 1904 in New York City and died in Kansas City, Missouri, in 1943. He was a pianist, organist, and composer whose jazz styles were rooted in stride, traditional, classic, and swing. Fats Waller was raised in a musical family and started playing piano at the age of six. He contributed such historic tunes as "Ain't Misbehavin'," "Jitterbug Waltz," "Keepin' Out of Mischief Now," "Handful of Keys," "I'm Gonna Sit Right Down and Write Myself a Letter," and "Honeysuckle Rose." Waller influenced such jazz greats as Count Basie, Art Tatum, Thelonious Monk, Teddy Wilson, and many others. Occasionally, bebop tunes such as "Scrapple from the Apple" were loosely based on the **ii-V** chord progressions used in "Honeysuckle Rose." Notice how repetition and syncopation play a big role in bebop-style progressions.

LICKS AND TRICKS

Lick #1 is a typical **ii-V** chord progression pattern. Lick #2 is another **ii-V** pattern; use this one on the final A section with the chord change modulating up a half step, adding a new harmonic opportunity for the soloist. Transpose these licks to all 12 keys! Lick #3 is a riff over the B section; continue this melodic pattern to each dominant chord in the bridge.

SCALES AND CHORDS

DISCOGRAPHY

HONEYSUCKLE ROSE
Fats Waller - *25 Greatest Hits* - Living Era (Koch) 5174
Louis Armstrong - *Satch Plays Fats* - Columbia 40378
Count Basie - *Swingsation* - GRP 9920

HONEYSUCKLE ROSE

CONDUCTOR'S NOTES

The tempo is 136 mm. "Honeysuckle Rose" is a swinging tune jam-packed with **ii-V** progressions offering more variety with a temporary half-step modulation in the last eight bars. This is a perfect opportunity to explore patterns, voicings and variations on the essential **ii-V** progression. Try playing this tune in different keys and it will open up your ears tremendously!

Piano:

- Try a moderately sustained style using the pedal very sparingly; contrast with a punctuated rhythmic style aiming to provide harmonic direction and color with rhythmic interest.
- This AABA song form jazz standard incorporates a temporary modulation in the last A section, and this gives a lift to the harmony. Enhance this lift by changing registers on the piano.
- The three suggested rhythms for comping example patterns provided are derived from rhythms played in the head. Try creating similar patterns on your own.
- Keep the voicings fairly simple using about 4–6 notes, and stay within the texture of the tune.
- Remember that the 3rd and 7th give the harmonic identity.

Bass:

- Create a smooth walking line.
- Keep it simple and always establish the harmonic foundation.
- The melodic content, known as voice leading, is a critical role of the bass player and a function you should continually be aware of. The bass player and ride cymbal must lock in.
- During the half-step temporary modulation in the last A section, establish the new tonal center by playing the root of the chord on the downbeat of each chord change. Fill in other beats with chord and scale tones.

Drums:

- Try a cross-stick on four behind soloists to establish a comfortable groove.
- Keep in mind that the written break-out drum part is only a general guide.
- A relaxed ride cymbal pattern with the hi-hat on two and four will work great.
- Always think about playing the form.
- Listen to the soloists for sequences and support rhythmic ideas they create.
- Most important: have fun!

Guitar:

This style of the guitar comping can be as complex as a series of punctuated chords or as simple as a repetitive pattern of quarter notes known as the "Freddie Green" sound. This style uses a closed or stopped sound with no sustain. Freddie Green was a legendary acoustic guitar player who performed with Count Basie and perfected the definitive acoustic guitar sound. As steady as any drummer's beat, Freddie Green's guitar sound was felt more than heard. He never overpowered the rhythm section or the piano. Especially with today's typical guitarist using electric guitar equipment, you must listen, learn and imitate this distinctive acoustic style.

- When called for, the jazz guitarist should strive to sound like an acoustic guitar.
- Always share the comping space with the piano player. (Listen and learn to avoid playing the same thing.)
- Alternate with the piano and be careful to play the same chord progressions at the turnarounds.
- Always work *with* the piano player, not *against*. Stay in the mid-range of the instrument using primarily the top four strings.

MAIDEN VOYAGE

LISTEN AND ANALYZE HEAD — Track 7 JAZZ DEMO

PLAY THE HEAD — Track 8 PLAY ALONG

PIANO

LATIN ROCK

BY HERBIE HANCOCK

SOLO SECTION - 2 CHORUSES
SUGGESTED VOICINGS FOR COMPING

SUGGESTED RHYTHM FOR COMPING

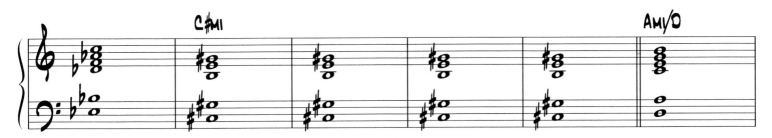

AFTER LAST SOLO
D.S. % AL CODA

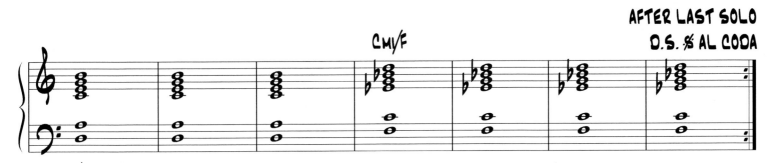

EXAMPLE IMPROVISATION
LISTEN AND ANALYZE
(JAZZ DEMO PLAYS 1 CHORUS)

C INSTRUMENTS

LATIN ROCK

BY WILLIE THOMAS

IMPROVISED SOLO
LISTEN, ANALYZE AND TRANSCRIBE Track 7
JAZZ DEMO
(JAZZ DEMO PLAYS 1 CHORUS)

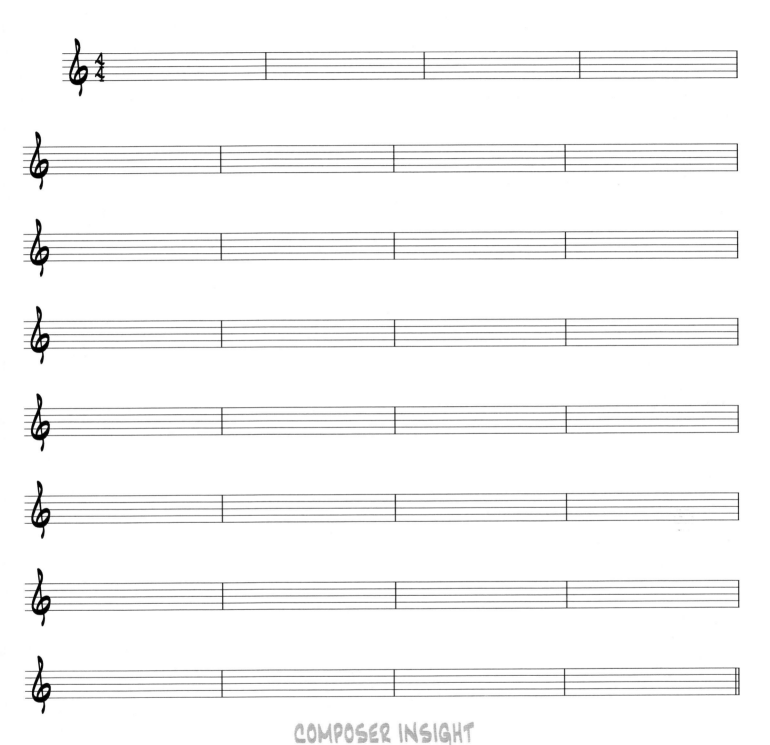

COMPOSER INSIGHT
MAIDEN VOYAGE

Written in an AABA 32-bar song form, Herbie Hancock's "Maiden Voyage" has become a very important part of the jazz musician's repertoire. Recorded in 1965 on the Blue Note label, it included stellar jazz masters Herbie Hancock (piano), Ron Carter (bass), Tony Williams (drums), George Coleman (tenor saxophone), and Freddie Hubbard (trumpet). A modal tune with sparse chord changes moving every four measures along with a repetitive rhythmical pattern in the melody makes this tune easy to memorize. The Dorian minor scale, the dominant scale sound, or a combination of the two may be used throughout. Developing skill in some of the more uncommon keys and chord progressions will be necessary for successful improvisation on this tune.

LICKS AND TRICKS

Lick #1, a four-measure chordal pattern, is written over the first two chord changes; transpose this pattern to the other chords. Lick #2 is a melodic and rhythmic pattern incorporating the ninth over the first two chord changes; transpose to the other chords. Lick #3 is a melodic riff written over the first two chord changes; transpose to the other chords.

SCALES AND CHORDS

DISCOGRAPHY

MAIDEN VOYAGE
Herbie Hancock - *Maiden Voyage* - Blue Note 95331
Herbie Hancock - *Best Of Herbie Hancock (The Blue Note Years)* - Blue Note 91142
GRP Big Band - *GRP All-Star Big Band* - GRP 9672

MAIDEN VOYAGE

CONDUCTOR'S NOTES

The tempo is 110 mm. This Herbie Hancock classic gives the players an opportunity to play within a fixed rhythmical pattern. This pattern continues throughout the tune; therefore, the rhythm section must play together with consistency and accuracy yet provide a loose and comfortable foundation for the ensemble. The drummer has opportunities to embellish the rhythmical pattern. Although the minor ninth chord is used throughout in the harmonic voicings, some color variation can be used. Listen to the CD for reference to this concept.

Piano:

- It is critical to play this written rhythmic and harmonic pattern throughout the tune, especially during the head of the tune.
- The piano and entire rhythm section in this jazz standard should keep the straight-eighth feel as opposed to a swing feel.
- Behind the soloists, you can add color with some inversions of the chords, but you should continue to play the established rhythmical pattern throughout.
- During the piano solo, you can depart from the established pattern and allow the guitarist to play the pattern.
- Try an electronic keyboard for color variety.

Bass:

- The bass line is locked into the written pattern in this tune.
- During the solo section, experiment with different octaves that may offer some contrast; however, continue playing in the same groove.
- As you will hear on the CD, the feel is straight eighths, not swing or a walking bass line.

Drums:

- Play with consistent energy throughout this tune.
- Note that the written break-out drum part is only a general guide. Listen to the CD!
- As the intensity builds, a strong groove can be reinforced with a cross-stick on the rim on all four beats. This will add strength and energy to the groove.
- As the solos progress, the drummer can embellish the fixed rhythm pattern while keeping the pattern accents intact. This will give a more open feeling; however, don't think of this as a drum solo, just as contrast.
- As always, complement, do not overpower, the others in the rhythm section. You can control ensemble dynamics!

Guitar:

- Feel free to play rhythmically active, and contrast (but do not conflict) with the piano pattern.
- The guitar can be more aggressive in this type of tune, but don't overpower.
- Different voicings and positions can add variety your sound.
- The use of some simple effects may also be incorporated here; however, always listen and communicate with the rest of the section for a solid rhythm section sound.

PIANO

JUST SQUEEZE ME

LISTEN AND ANALYZE HEAD   Track 9   JAZZ DEMO

PLAY THE HEAD   Track 10   PLAY ALONG

EASY SWING   BY DUKE ELLINGTON

Suggested Rhythms For Comping

SOLO SECTION – 2 CHORUSES
SUGGESTED VOICINGS FOR COMPING

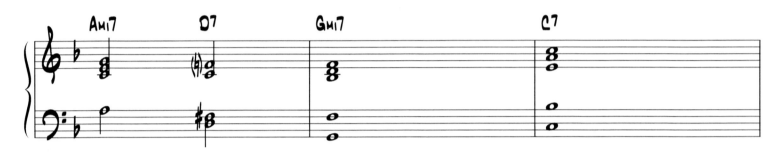

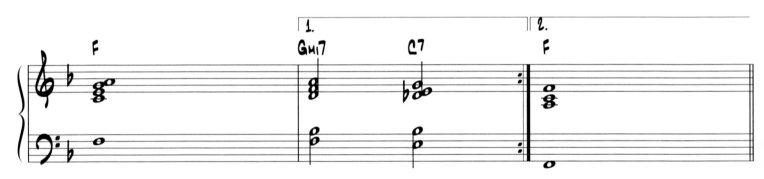

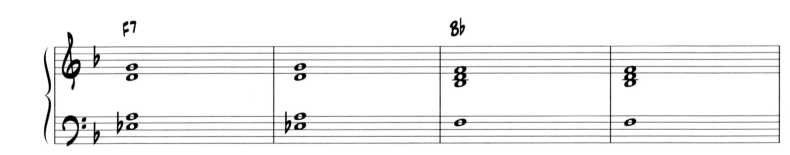

AFTER LAST SOLO D.S. ℅ AL CODA

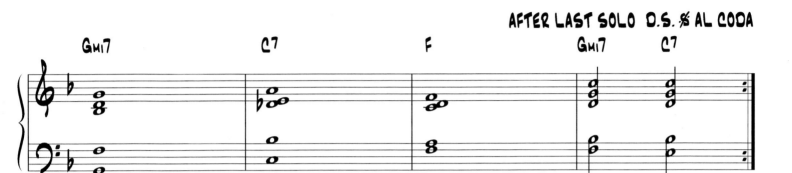

EXAMPLE IMPROVISATION
LISTEN AND ANALYZE

Track 9
JAZZ DEMO

(JAZZ DEMO PLAYS 1 CHORUS)

BY RON JOLLY

C INSTRUMENTS

IMPROVISED SOLO
LISTEN, ANALYZE AND TRANSCRIBE
(JAZZ DEMO PLAYS 1 CHORUS)

Track 9
JAZZ DEMO

COMPOSER INSIGHT

JUST SQUEEZE ME

This tune is an AABA 32-bar song by Edward Kennedy "Duke" Ellington, born April 29, 1899, in Washington, D.C., and died May 24, 1974, in New York City. He was a composer, bandleader, and pianist who will be remembered as one of the greatest jazz artists and composers of the twentieth century. When one thinks of the big band era or the swing era, it is synonymous with Duke Ellington and his orchestra. Between 1926 and 1974 was the period of greatness of this genius. It was during this time that Ellington wrote such wonderful compositions as "East St. Louis Toodle-oo," "Black and Tan Fantasy," "I Let a Song Go Out of My Heart," "Prelude to a Kiss," "Don't Get Around Much Anymore," and "Just Squeeze Me." Ellington's "Just Squeeze Me" was written during the 1940s while he was performing his annual concerts at Carnegie Hall in New York City. This is a simple but fun tune with an interesting diatonic chord pattern in the A section and a bridge progression of dominant 7th chords.

C INSTRUMENTS

Lick #1 shows a chordal pattern outlining the diatonic chord progression in the A section. Lick #2 offers a rhythmic pattern over the diatonic chord progression. Lick #3 is a lick designed to work over the bridge or B section changes; continue this pattern over each dominant 7th chord.

SCALES AND CHORDS

JUST SQUEEZE ME
Duke Ellington/Johnny Hodges - *Side By Side* - Verve 521405
Louis Armstrong - *Satch Plays Fats* - Columbia 40378
Paul Desmond - *The Best Of Paul Desmond* - Columbia 45484
Louis Armstrong & Duke Ellington - Roulette CDP 7938442

JUST SQUEEZE ME

The tempo is 108 mm. A relaxed medium swing, this fairly simple standard should be easy to pull together. Much of this harmonic content is diatonic or related to the scale of the tonic key (in this case F). Notice that the bridge offers more harmonic contrast. Simplicity is the essence of this type of tune; less is better.

Piano:

- The introduction to "Just Squeeze Me" is unison with the bass. The tendency is to rush this tempo—relax and keep the time feeling comfortable.
- Accompaniment should be fairly sparse on this standard. Check out the Count Basie style of piano playing; it's focused on punctuated rhythms and the use of space. It is essential listening.
- The three suggested rhythms for comping example patterns provided are derived from rhythms played in the head. Use these patterns or experiment on your own.
- Use these comping patterns individually or try playing all the patterns together as one phrase.
- Check out the suggested voicings; notice that the harmonic sound or quality is determined by the 3rd and 7th, not the root and 5th.

Bass:

- This standard tune offers you a challenge to keep up the tempo and yet still keep a relaxed and comfortable feel to the bass part.
- To create a relaxed groove and still keep the forward motion of time, you must concentrate or the tempo may slip.
- A smooth walking bass line is a must here, especially at the ascending/descending patterns.
- Keep it simple and always establish the harmonic foundation.
- The bass player and the ride cymbal must lock in.
- A rhythmical variation such as triplets or eighth-note groups should be used sparingly.

Drums:

- Remember that the written drum part is only a break-out guide.
- Cross-stick on four will work nicely in this groove with some minimal fills at each turnaround.
- This tempo certainly needs to swing, but still maintain a relaxed feel. Balance the energy flow.
- Fill during the introduction, but keep it simple.
- As always, complement, do not overpower, the others in the rhythm section. You can control ensemble dynamics!

Guitar:

- Flat-four feel à la Freddie Green works great here. (Refer to the guitar notes in "Honeysuckle Rose.")
- During the solo comping, always be sensitive to the piano and share the musical space. Keep the sound warm and mellow throughout.
- Relax and keep steady time with your comping. Less is better.
- You can reinforce the walk-up progression in the first few bars of the melody.

PIANO

CARAVAN

LISTEN AND ANALYZE HEAD  Track 11
JAZZ DEMO

PLAY THE HEAD  Track 12
PLAY ALONG

By JUAN TIZOL

AFRO-CUBAN
INTRO

Fmi

SUGGESTED RHYTHMS FOR COMPING

Pattern A.) Pattern B.) Pattern C.)

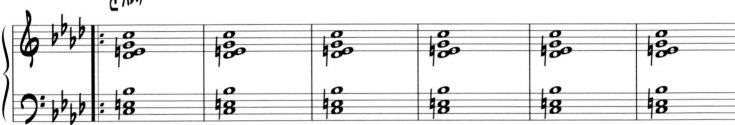

SOLO SECTION - 2 CHORUSES
SUGGESTED VOICINGS FOR COMPING

Track 12
PLAY ALONG

AFRO-CUBAN
C7(b9)

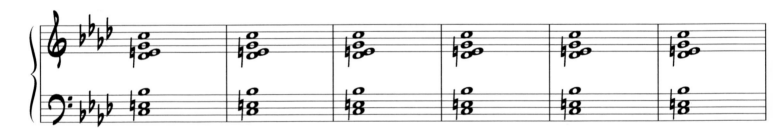

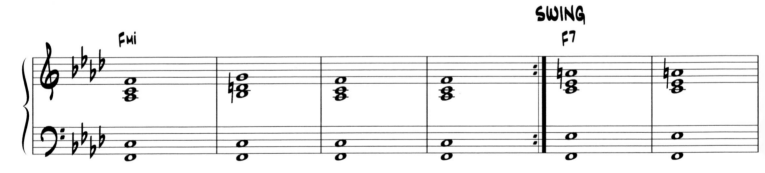

Fmi

SWING
F7

Bb7

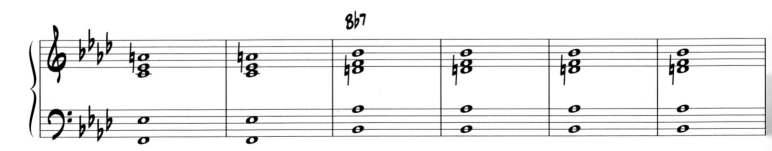

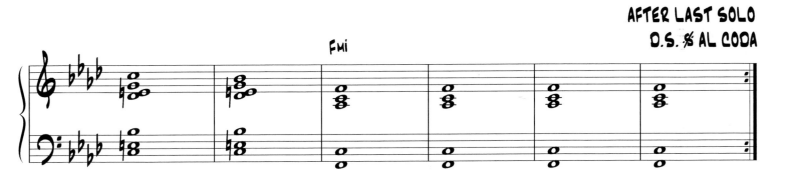

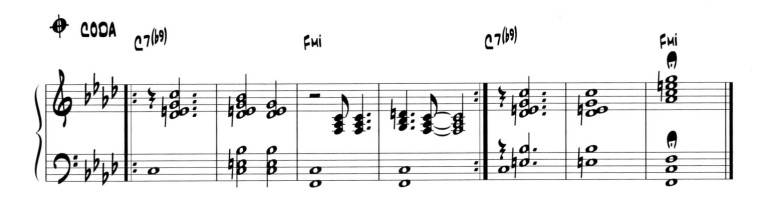

41

EXAMPLE IMPROVISATION
LISTEN AND ANALYZE
(JAZZ DEMO PLAYS 1 CHORUS)

Track 11
JAZZ DEMO

BY JAVON JACKSON

C INSTRUMENTS

C INSTRUMENTS

IMPROVISED SOLO
LISTEN, ANALYZE AND TRANSCRIBE

Track 11
JAZZ DEMO

(JAZZ DEMO PLAYS 1 CHORUS)

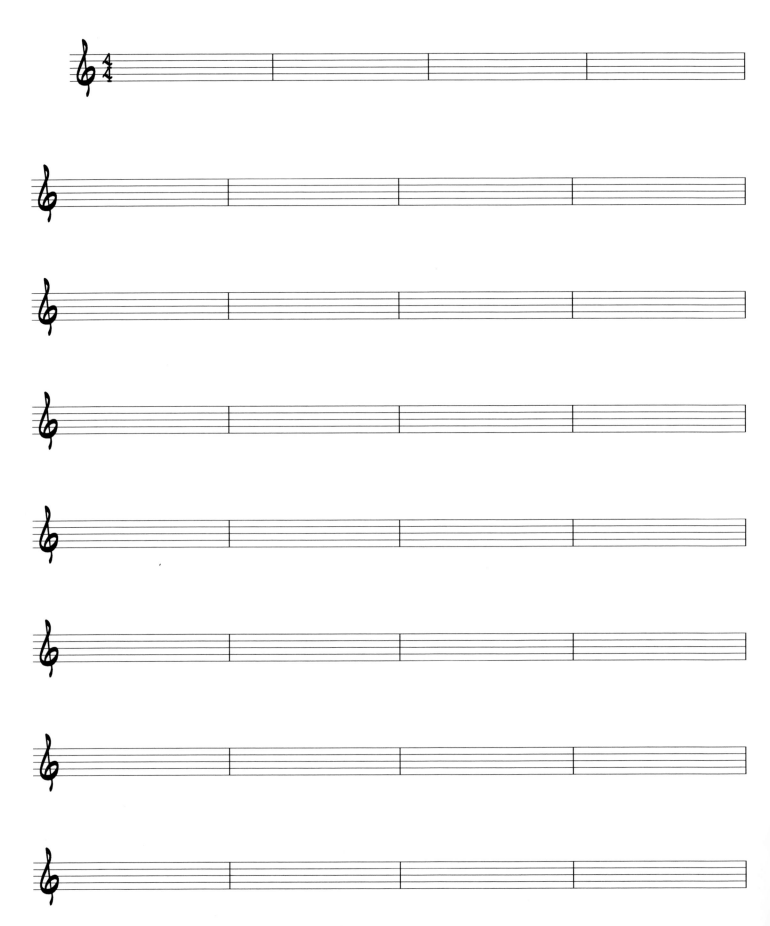

C INSTRUMENTS

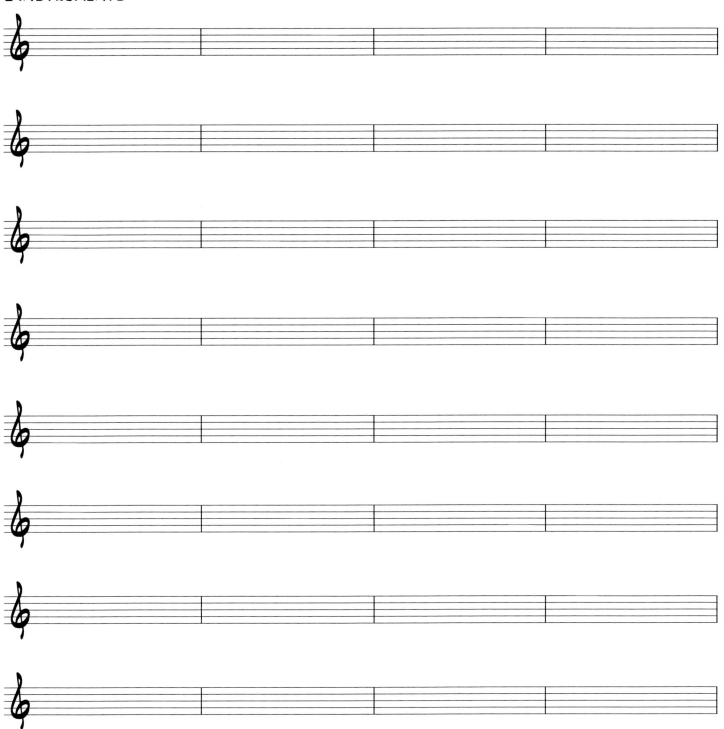

COMPOSER INSIGHT

CARAVAN

Juan Tizol penned this AABA 32-bar song. He was born in 1900 in San Juan, Puerto Rico, and died in 1984 in Inglewood, California. He played the valve trombone and was a very important composer and arranger for the Duke Ellington Orchestra from 1929 to 1944. Tizol composed such hit tunes as "Conga Brava," "Moonlight Fiesta," "Perdido," and "Caravan." He was a member of the Ellington Orchestra when he wrote "Caravan" in 1937. This exciting standard is laced with interesting possibilities to improvise. Traditionally this tune is rhythmically played with the A section Afro-Cuban and the bridge in a swing style. Since the use of non-chord tones adds color and interest throughout, take advantage of this opportunity to explore these colors, especially during the 12 bars of the ♭9 chord.

C INSTRUMENTS

LICKS AND TRICKS

Lick #1 is a diminished scale pattern; continue throughout the full range of your instrument. Lick #2 is simply a chromatic scale pattern; continue throughout the full range of your instrument. Lick #3 is a melodic and rhythmic pattern over the B section; continue this pattern over each dominant chord in the bridge.

SCALES AND CHORDS

C INSTRUMENTS

DISCOGRAPHY

CARAVAN
Duke Ellington - *Priceless Jazz Collection* - GRP 9875
Duke Ellington - *Soul Call* - Verve 539785
Wes Montgomery - *Ultimate Wes Montgomery* - Verve 539787
Freddie Hubbard - *The Artistry Of Freddie Hubbard* - GRP 179
The Best Of Duke Ellington - Capitol 7243 8 31501

CARAVAN

The tempo is 196 mm. This is an important tune to learn and know how to play. Even though the tune is in four, the Afro-Cuban section has a two feel. The tendency is to rush the swing section—hold back. There are 12 bars of the C7($\flat$9) chord in the A section that offer a good opportunity to use a technique known as harmonic tension and release. Use the minor ninth interval in the C7($\flat$9) (C-D$\flat$) for the tension or dissonance, and then release or resolve this dissonance at the F minor chord.

Piano:

- Think rhythmically during the first 12 bars of the C7 and keep the energy flowing—not necessarily a lot of notes, just rhythmical accents and punctuation. The extreme is to play too much; don't fill every musical space.
- Use the tension-and-release technique discussed above. Don't be afraid of the minor ninth or minor second interval.
- The swing bridge gives you a chance to change styles completely.
- Vary the register and inversion of the chords to sustain harmonic interest and energy to your comping.
- Unison octaves is another technique. Listen to the CD for ideas.
- Alternate with the guitar for color change in the solo comping section.

Bass:

- The bass line is locked into the written pattern in the A section in this tune. Keep it simple and work on establishing the harmonic foundation.
- Walk that bridge!
- During the solos, consider experimenting with simple embellishments to the rhythmic pattern; however, keep the same groove.
- As you will hear on the CD, there should be a two-feel in the Afro-Cuban sections; then swing hard in four with a walking bass line on the bridge. The Afro-Cuban feel is essential to your repertoire—listen and learn it.
- Always lock in with the drummer.

Drums:

- Play with drive throughout this tune.
- Note that the written break-out drum part is only a general guide.
- Listen to the CD! Learn the Afro-Cuban feel and style. Use the toms.
- A strong back-beat or cross-stick on four on the bridge will give energy to the swing feel.
- As always, complement, do not overpower, the others in the rhythm section. Control ensemble dynamics!
- Record the ensemble to listen to your playing to analyze and critique yourself.
- Try using the ride cymbal crown for color on the Afro-Cuban section.

Guitar:

- Feel free to play rhythmically active, and contrast (but don't conflict) with the piano pattern.
- The guitar can be more aggressive in this type of tune.
- Different voicings and positions can add variety your sound—experiment.
- The rhythm section must wear two musical hats in this tune: a free and open Afro-Cuban section with lots of rhythmic variety and contrast, and then swing with a steady traditional comping rhythm style.

THIS PAGE HAS BEEN LEFT BLANK TO
FACILITATE PAGE TURNS.

PIANO

IN A MELLOW TONE

LISTEN AND ANALYZE HEAD

PLAY THE HEAD

Track 13
JAZZ DEMO

Track 14
PLAY ALONG

BY DUKE ELLINGTON

MEDIUM SWING
INTRO

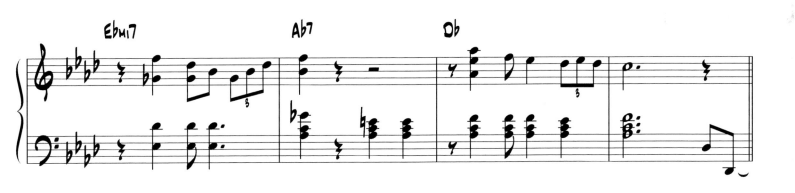

SUGGESTED RHYTHMS FOR COMPING

Pattern A.) **Pattern B.)** **Pattern C.)**

SOLO SECTION -2 CHORUSES
SUGGESTED VOICINGS FOR COMPING

Track 14
PLAY ALONG

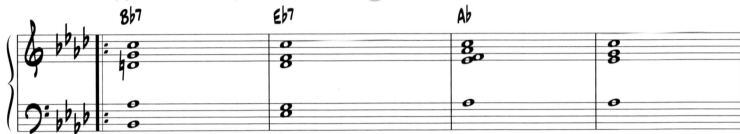

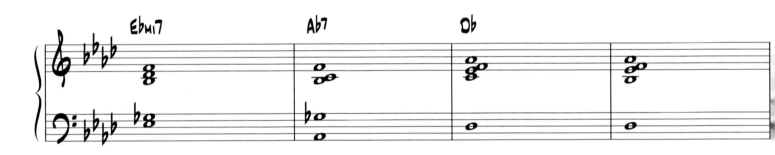

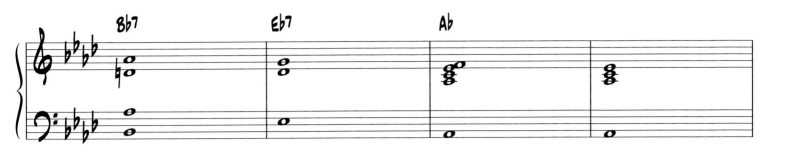

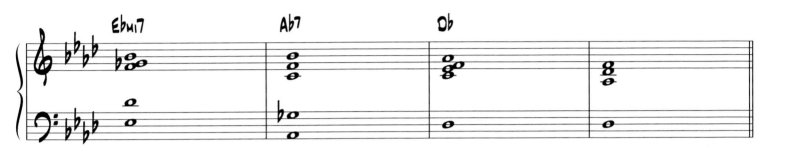

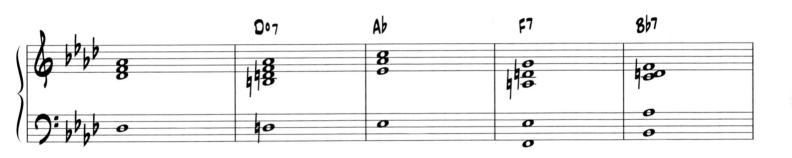

C INSTRUMENTS

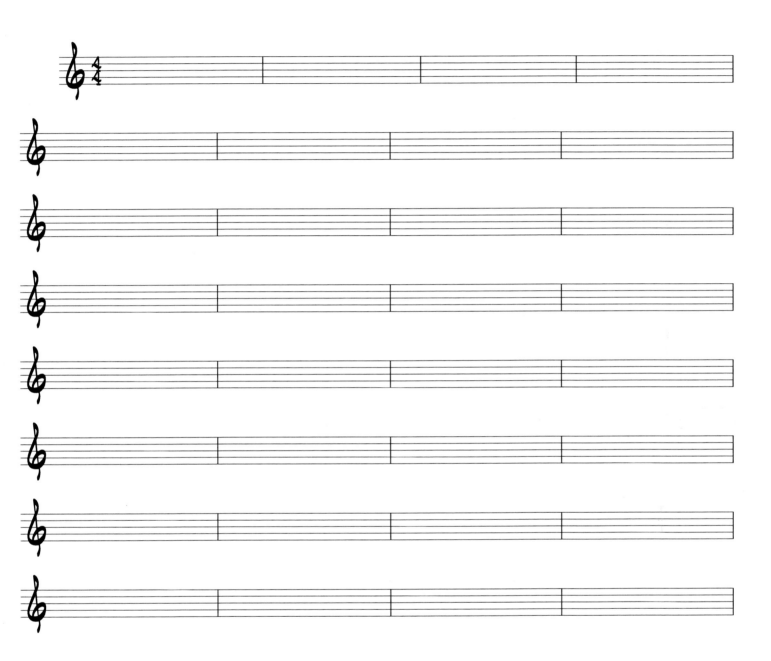

COMPOSER INSIGHT

IN A MELLOW TONE

"In a Mellow Tone," an AB 32-bar song written in 1940, is another classic by Edward Kennedy "Duke" Ellington that has become part of the jazz repertoire. It was during this period that the Ellington band was at its peak of recording activity. The band recorded "Chelsea Bridge," "Perdido," "Take the 'A' Train," "Cotton Tail," "Concerto for Cootie," and many others to etch its place in jazz history as one of the greatest jazz entities to ever exist. Born in 1899 in Washington, D.C., and died May 24, 1974, in New York City, composer/arranger/pianist/bandleader Duke considered the orchestra his main instrument. He will certainly be remembered as one of the greatest composers of the twentieth century. "In a Mellow Tone" is aptly titled as a relaxed and easy-going tune, but it keeps you thinking with the use of many dominant chords and a diminished chord.

Lick #1 begins with a melodic lick outlining the major **ii-V-I** chord progression in measures 1–4 of the melody. Lick #2 is a melodic pattern outlining another **ii-V-I** progression in measures 5–8 of the melody. Lick #3 is a rhythmic pattern outlining the diminished chord pattern in measures 25–28.

SCALES AND CHORDS

DISCOGRAPHY

IN A MELLOW TONE
Duke Ellington - *Blues In Orbit* - Columbia 44051
Louis Armstrong/Duke Ellington - *The Complete Sessions* - Roulette 93844
Ellington Orchestra With Mercer Ellington - *Digital Duke* - GRP 9548
Kenny Burrell - *Ellington Is Forever, Vol. 2* - Fantasy 79008

IN A MELLOW TONE

The tempo is 108 mm. *Mellow* is the keyword here. To maintain a nice, easy groove, this chord progression demands that the rhythm section work together. Ellington composed this tune rather deceptively. It looks and feels easy to play initially, but you must concentrate or risk getting lost very easily. The diminished chord is a nice hook.

Piano:

- This easy swing style tune moves along leisurely, but you can add energy by short rhythmic backgrounds.
- To add variety behind the solos, play occasional sustained figures to contrast the short punctuated comping ideas.
- The diminished chord is a nice hook that "Mellow Tone" offers in addition to the frequent **ii-V** chord progressions.
- The three suggested rhythms for comping example patterns provided are derived from rhythms played in the head. Use these patterns or experiment on your own.
- Try the comping patterns using the individual patterns or the entire five-bar pattern as one idea.
- Fill with some simple single-note lines with the right hand.

Bass:

- Observe the walking up or down to the next chord because it makes the bass line smooth and directs the band into the next chord. This is called voice leading.
- Remember to play the root of the chord change on the downbeat.
- In this standard, you will notice the written bass part avoids any extremely high range and does not linger on any particular note, especially the fourth of a scale.
- The bassist should always lock in with the drummer.

Drums:

- In this jazz style, the drummer should complement or enhance the music, not overpower or dominate.
- The drummer has a few fills in the intro of the tune; after that, it's smooth sailing with basic time or the break-out pattern for swing.
- The break-out pattern is only a general guide to what the drummer should play.
- Listen carefully to the CD recording to get a sense of how the drummer interprets the basic swing patterns.
- Use various cymbals to contrast and refresh the sound, perhaps changing cymbals for each new soloist. Use a cross-stick on beat 4 during the solo section.

Guitar:

- Flat-four feel à la Freddie Green works great here. (Refer to the guitar notes in "Honeysuckle Rose.")
- During the solo section comping, be sensitive to the piano and share the musical space. Keep the sound warm and mellow throughout.
- Alternate comping with the piano. Be careful to play the same chord progressions at the turnarounds.
- Always *work* with the piano player—not *against*. Stay in the mid-range of the instrument using primarily the top four strings

PERDIDO

LISTEN AND ANALYZE HEAD

PLAY THE HEAD

Track 15
JAZZ DEMO

Track 16
PLAY ALONG

BY COMPOSER

MEDIUM UP-TEMPO SWING

INTRO

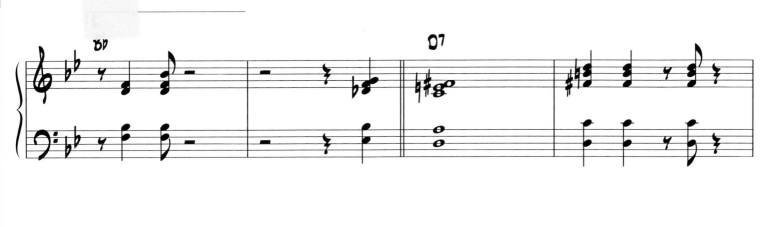

TO CODA ⊕

AFTER LAST SOLO
D.S. ‰ AL CODA

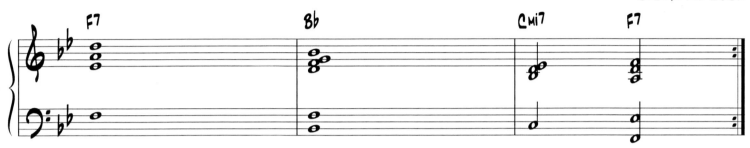

⊕ CODA

EXAMPLE IMPROVISATION
LISTEN AND ANALYZE
(JAZZ DEMO PLAYS 1 CHORUS)

Track 15
JAZZ DEMO

BY RON JOLLY

COMPOSER INSIGHT

PERDIDO

This AABA 32-bar song was written by Juan Tizol, born in 1900 in San Juan, Puerto Rico, and died in 1984 in Inglewood, California. He was a very important musical entity of the Duke Ellington Orchestra for 15 years, from 1929 to 1944, as a valve trombonist and composer/arranger. After he arrived in the United States in 1920, Tizol worked with the Marie Lucas Orchestra, the White Brothers Band, and later the Ellington Orchestra, Harry James, and others. A few of his important compositions are "Bakiff," "Conga Brava," "Moonlight Fiesta," and "Caravan." "Perdido" is a well-known swing-era standard performed frequently at jazz concerts generally at a medium to fast tempo in the key of B♭. With few complex rhythmic challenges, the player can focus on the chord progressions. Note that the B section has a dominant 7th chord progression cycle.

LICKS AND TRICKS

Lick #1 uses a typical **ii-V** pattern. Lick #2 is a turn-around pattern you can use in measures 7–8, which leads back into the minor **ii** chord at the beginning of the A section. Lick #3 is a **ii-V** pattern with non-harmonic tones.

SCALES AND CHORDS

PERDIDO

Duke Ellington - *Best Of The Duke Ellington Centennial Edition* - RCA Victor 63459
Ellington Orchestra With Mercer Ellington - *Digital Duke* - GRP9548
Coleman Hawkins - *Hawkins, Eldridge, Hodges Alive! At The Village Gate* - Verve 513755

64

PERDIDO

The tempo is 150 mm. It's very important that students work this tune from every angle. The AABA 32-bar song form is one of the most common forms in music, and this one swings all the way! Students can explore the frequent **ii-V-I** chord progressions in the first 16 bars and then experiment with the blues scale during the bridge, which consists of dominant chord cycles: D7, G7, C7, F7. Students should transcribe, memorize and absorb various jazz masters' interpretations of this chord progression and form. When the students are ready, try playing this in a different key!

Piano:

- Use a short, punctuated style of comping on this tune.
- While comping behind the soloists, vary the rhythmic pattern and harmonic voicings.
- Use of the 6th and 9th will add color to the chord while the 3rd and 7th will dictate the overall sound or identity of the chord.
- During the B section, vary the rhythmic patterns with more a sustained comping style to provide contrast.
- The three Suggested Rhythms for Comping example patterns provided are derived from rhythms played in the head. Use these patterns or experiment on your own.
- You can use each comping pattern individually or play them together as one extended pattern.

Bass:

- Your job is a tough one because you must provide rhythmic and harmonic foundation simultaneously.
- Walk the time with consistent quarter notes giving the traditional swing sound and feel, and try to connect the chord progressions with clear voice leading and a logical bass line. This will guide the harmonic direction and establish the tonal center. Listen to the CD!
- At this tempo, keep on top of the time and try to think together with the drummer.

Drums:

- The ride cymbal along with the hi-hat should provide the basic time at this tempo. Listen to the CD.
- During the B section or bridge, contrast and vary with different cymbals. Try changing the cymbal sound with each soloist.
- Play the snare for kicks and hits that are quarter notes or shorter, and play the bass, drum and cymbal for longer kicks.
- Keep the fills simple, always stay on top of the time and be aware of the potential to drag or slow down.
- As always, the break-out written drum part is only a general guide.
- During the solo section, try a cross-stick on four; it will add to the energy at this tempo.

Guitar:

- Playing on all four beats à la Freddie Green (refer to guitar notes for "Honeysuckle Rose") works fine, but add some mid-range rhythmic punctuation as well.
- Different voicings or positions can add variety to your sound and to the texture of the ensemble.
- Catch the rhythms with the piano during the introduction.
- Try alternating choruses with the piano for a contrast in color and texture.
- Soloing on this tune will be fun; try to keep a more traditional mellow jazz tone on your instrument.

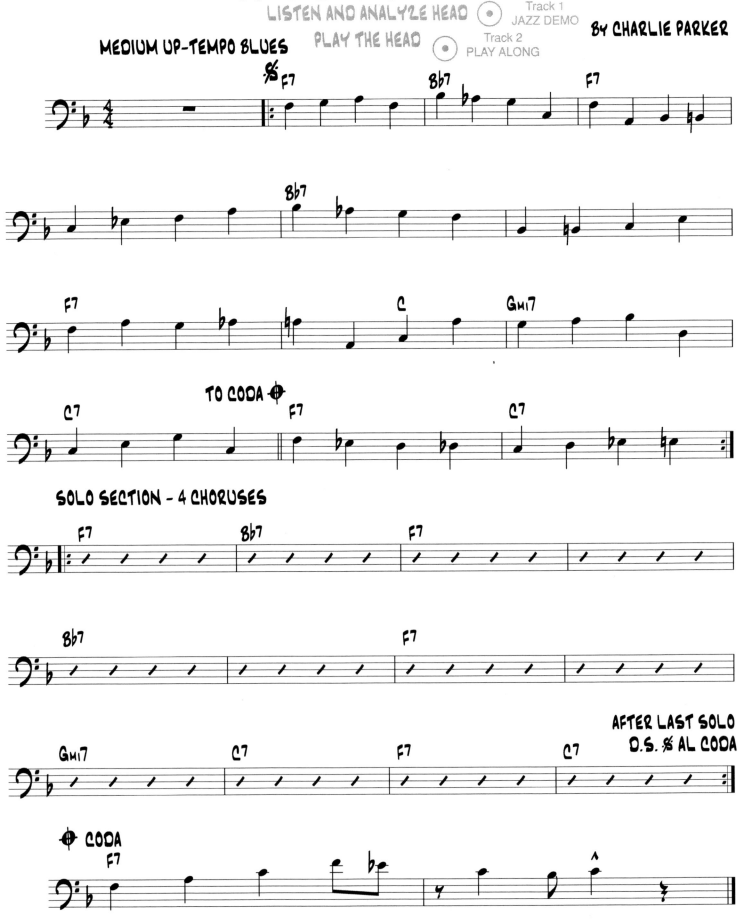

HONEYSUCKLE ROSE

Bass

LISTEN AND ANALYZE HEAD   Track 5   JAZZ DEMO

PLAY THE HEAD   Track 6   PLAY ALONG

BY FATS WALLER

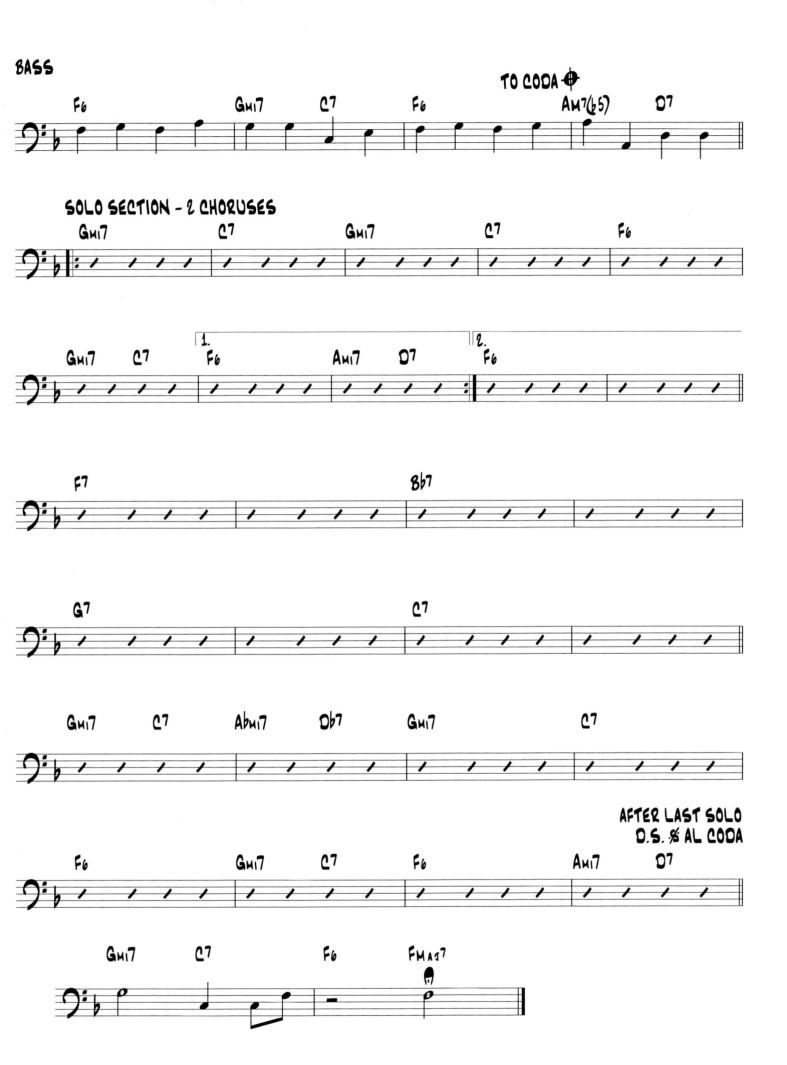

MAIDEN VOYAGE

LISTEN AND ANALYZE HEAD — Track 7 JAZZ DEMO

PLAY THE HEAD — Track 8 PLAY ALONG

BY HERBIE HANCOCK

BASS

LATIN ROCK

BASS

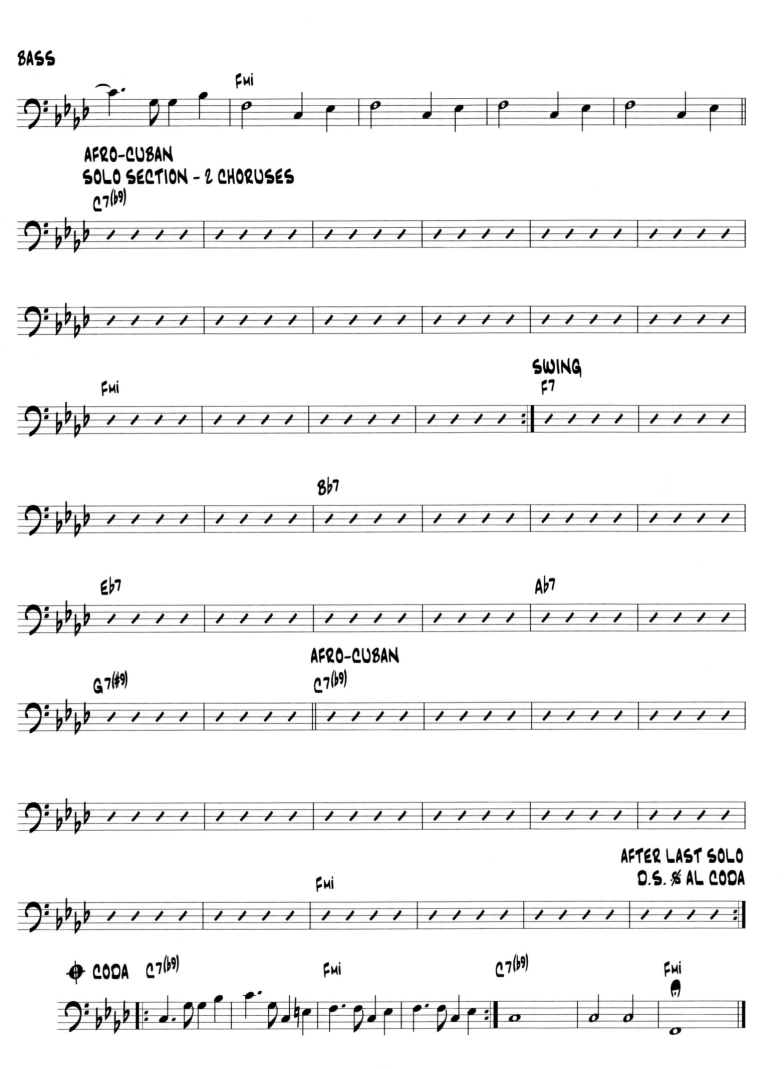

In a Mellow Tone

BASS

LISTEN AND ANALYZE HEAD — Track 13 JAZZ DEMO
PLAY THE HEAD — Track 14 PLAY ALONG

BY DUKE ELLINGTON

MEDIUM SWING
INTRO

PERDIDO

LISTEN AND ANALYZE HEAD — Track 15 JAZZ DEMO

PLAY THE HEAD — Track 16 PLAY ALONG

BY JUAN TIZOL

BASS

BASS

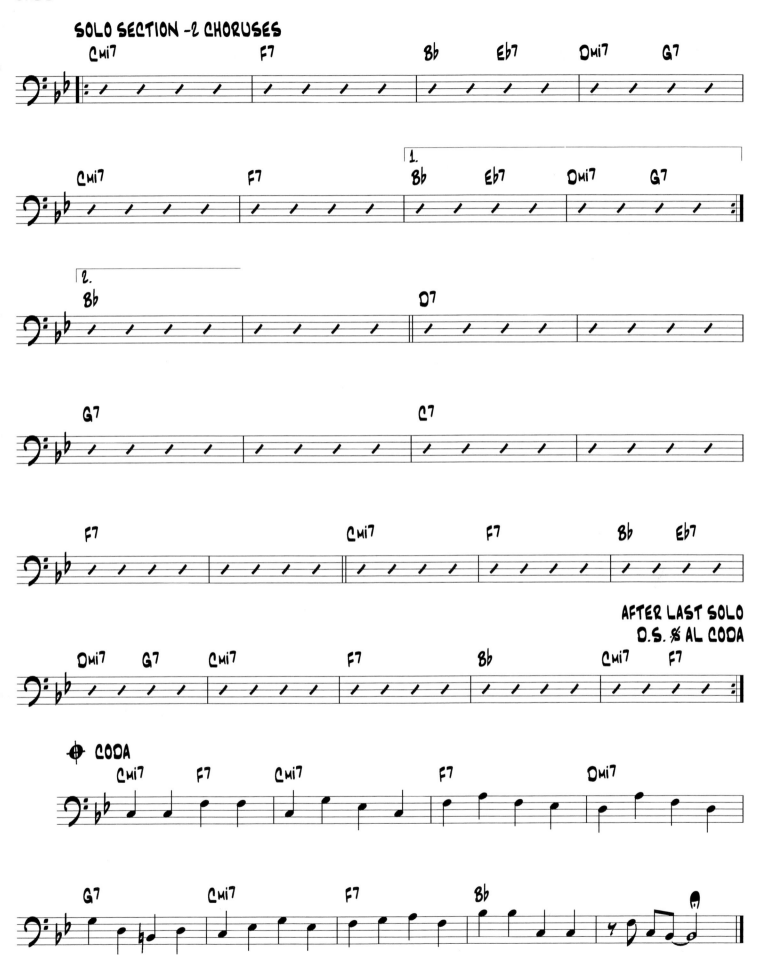

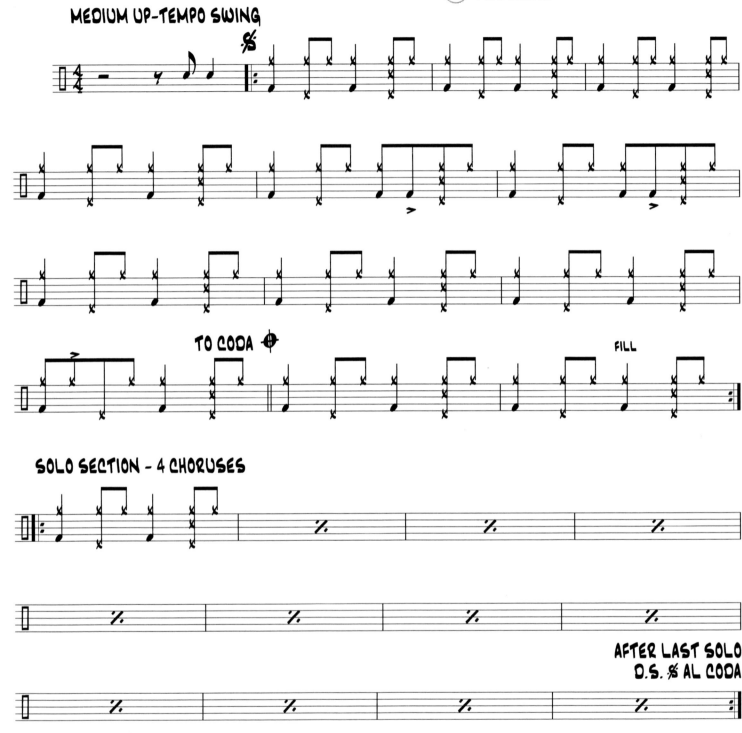

Drums

SUGAR

LISTEN AND ANALYZE HEAD ⦿ Track 3
                                JAZZ DEMO
PLAY THE HEAD ⦿ Track 4
                   PLAY ALONG

BY STANLEY TURRENTINE

MEDIUM SHUFFLE

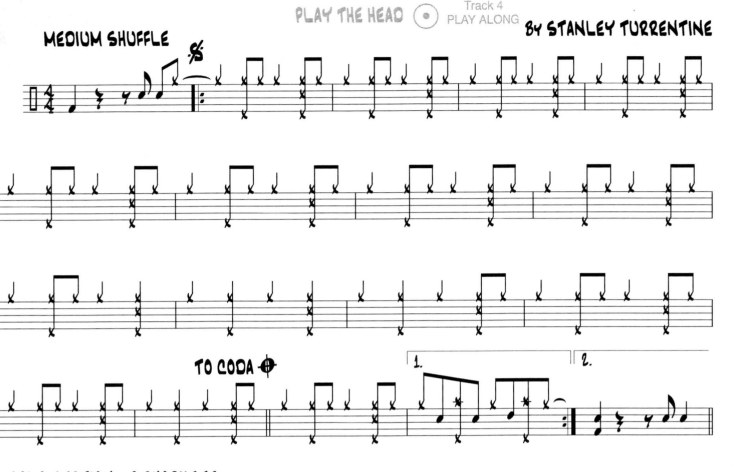

TO CODA ⊕

1.

2.

SOLO SECTION - 2 CHORUSES

AFTER LAST SOLO
D.S. ℅ AL CODA

⊕ CODA

FILL   FILL

HONEYSUCKLE ROSE

LISTEN AND ANALYZE HEAD — Track 5 JAZZ DEMO

PLAY THE HEAD — Track 6 PLAY ALONG

BY FATS WALLER

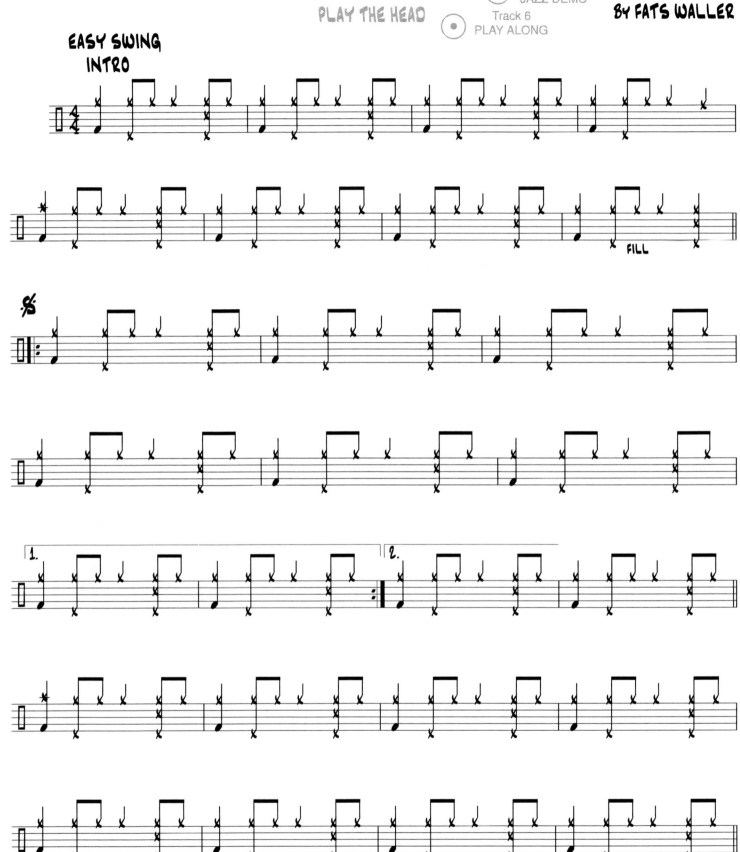

DRUMS

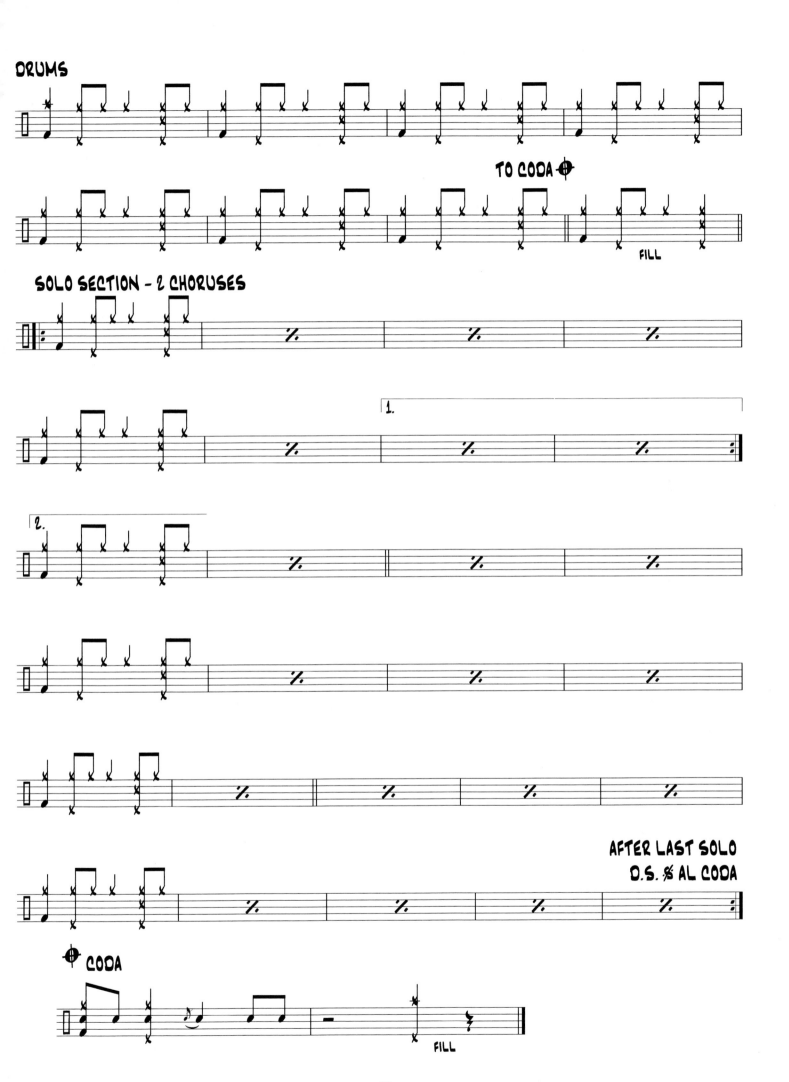

TO CODA

SOLO SECTION - 2 CHORUSES

FILL

1.

2.

AFTER LAST SOLO
D.S. % AL CODA

CODA

FILL

83

MAIDEN VOYAGE

DRUMS

LATIN ROCK

LISTEN AND ANALYZE HEAD — Track 7 JAZZ DEMO

PLAY THE HEAD — Track 8 PLAY ALONG

BY HERBIE HANCOCK

TO CODA

DRUMS

SOLO SECTION - 2 CHORUSES

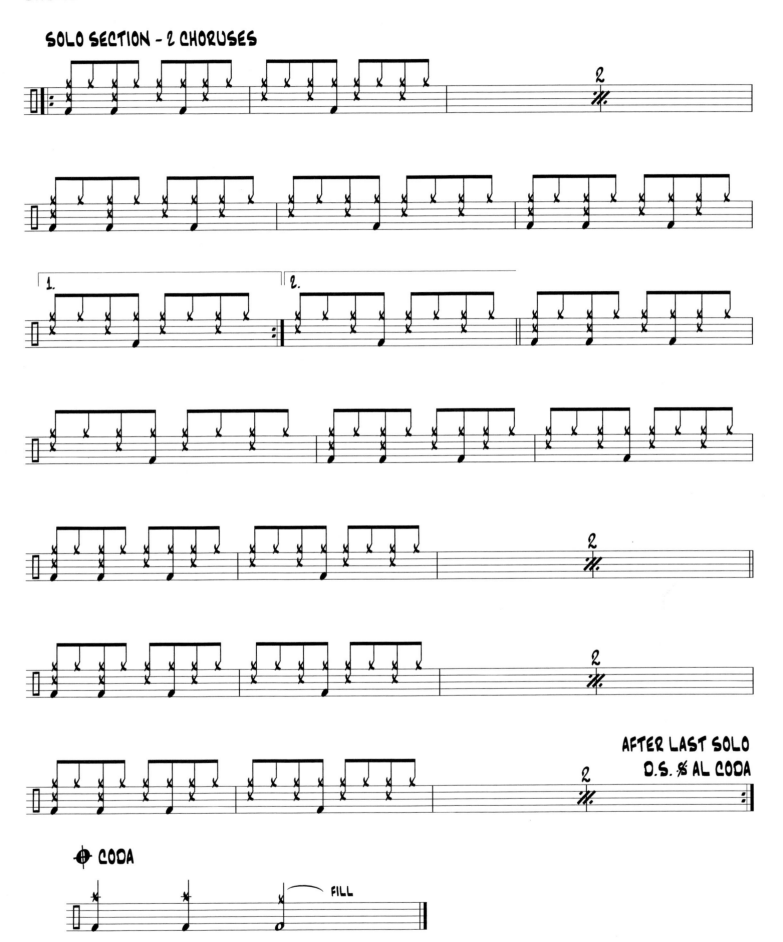

Drums

Just Squeeze Me

LISTEN AND ANALYZE HEAD ⊙ Track 9 JAZZ DEMO

PLAY THE HEAD ⊙ Track 10 PLAY ALONG

BY DUKE ELLINGTON

DRUMS

SOLO SECTION - 2 CHORUSES

AFTER LAST SOLO
D.S. % AL CODA

DRUMS

SOLO SECTION - 2 CHORUSES
AFRO-CUBAN

SWING

AFRO-CUBAN

AFTER LAST SOLO
D.S. % AL CODA

CODA

FILL

IN A MELLOW TONE

DRUMS

LISTEN AND ANALYZE HEAD — Track 13 JAZZ DEMO

PLAY THE HEAD — Track 14 PLAY ALONG

BY DUKE ELLINGTON

MEDIUM SWING
INTRO

TO CODA

DRUMS

SOLO SECTION - 2 CHORUSES

DRUMS

PERDIDO

LISTEN AND ANALYZE HEAD  Track 15 JAZZ DEMO

PLAY THE HEAD   Track 16 PLAY ALONG

BY JUAN TIZOL

DRUMS

SOLO SECTION - 2 CHORUSES

COMMON JAZZ IMPROVISING TERMS

ALTERED CHORD - A diatonic chord that has been altered by raising or lowering one or more of its elements (root, third, fifth, or seventh) a half step but has not changed the function or tonality.

BLUES SCALE - 1, ♭3, 4, ♯4, 5, ♭7 scale tones. No chord symbol.

BREAK-OUT PATTERN - A basic time pattern to be used as a general guide; the drummer can "break out" from this pattern and develop variations on this pattern.

BRIDGE - The B section of the AABA form, often called the release.

CHORD - Simultaneous sounding of three or more tones—1, 3, 5, 7 of scale.

CHORD PROGRESSION - Series of successive chords, which accompany the melody.

CHORUS - The form of the tune, or one time through the entire chord progression of the tune.

DIATONIC - An order of tones or intervals simply illustrated by the white keys of the piano; starting with C.

DIMINISHED SCALE - Eight-note scale with intervals consisting of WHWHWHWH.

DOMINANT 7TH CHORD - A major-minor seventh chord built on the fifth scale degree in either major or harmonic minor tonality: 1, 3, 5, ♭7.

LICK - A short musical idea or motive.

HALF DIMINISHED SCALE - Seven-note scale with intervals consisting of HWWHWWW.

HEAD - Melody.

IMPROVISATION - Creating musical ideas played over the chord progression. Scales, chords, rhythms, and tune melodies are guides.

NON-HARMONIC TONES - Outside the diatonic scale or key.

PATTERN - Also referred to as a segment, a short musical phrase repeated.

PENTATONIC SCALE - Five-note scale.

RIFF - Short musical idea repeated.

SEQUENCE - A systematic transposition of a motive to different scale degrees. It may be literal (modulating) or diatonic (non-modulating).

TONIC NOTE - Keynote of scale or first degree of scale.

WHOLE-TONE SCALE - Six-tone scale, each interval a whole step.

I, IV, V CHORDS, ETC. - Another more traditional way to notate chord progressions. This notation provides a broader perspective on chord relationships. Numeral refers to scale tone. Major = uppercase; minor = lowercase.

Standard Jazz Chord Voicings (The root is circled.)

* Do not play the root.